8/12/47

To George Hutchinson

Who is:

(a) the outstanding fly-line caster,
(b) the Bait-choosing expert
(c) the best picker of fishing holes
(d) the undaunted patient Waiter
(e) the Wader Supreme
(f) the expert at reeling
(G) the Woodsman
(i) the Connoisseur of
fishing strategy and
and (j) the prospective idol of
all fishing inebriants as soon as you

learn how to Catch Fish — Hank Dee Jimmy & Patti

TO HELL
WITH
FISHING

Life's Darkest Moment

TO HELL
WITH
FISHING

or

How to Tell Fish from Fishermen

by

H. T. WEBSTER and ED ZERN

Foreword by COREY FORD

D. APPLETON-CENTURY COMPANY, INC.
New York   London

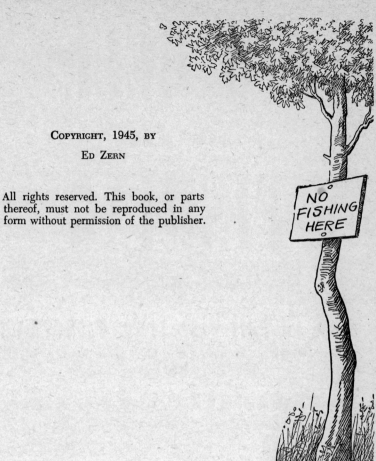

PRINTED IN THE UNITED STATES OF AMERICA

THIS BOOK IS DEDICATED TO

GOLLUP KUHN · PHILO CALHOUN · JAMES & JANE DEREN

D. A. SHAMBAUGH · LYMAN & MARY CLARK · HERB ROTH

MARVIN & GRACE CHASE · LEWIS H. BROWN

ENDERS M. VOORHEES · LARRY & PEGGY MADISON

JACK ROWLES · KURT LEHMAN · SEWARD WEBB

LOU CALDER · WALT & WINNIE DETTE · HILL HARRIS

BROOK ZERN · ETHEL WEBSTER · ROY DIGGANS

PAUL MOORE · MAURICE WERTHEIM · J. J. FISCHER

JOSE MARTIN · DICK JARMEL · ART BUTTERWICK

W. L. BRANN · JOHN T. MCCUTCHEON · CARL B. SPITZER

PIERCE MACNAIR · JOHN MARSH · SPARSE GREY HACKLE

CARL CLEVELAND · JIM BOLGER · HENRY SCHLICHTING

BERT SARGENT · RUSSELL PARRY · BILL SCHUSTER

ART WERNER · CY LIBERMAN · LEO KENNEDY

LARRY GOLOB · DICK MALTZ · BAIRD FOSTER

WILLIAM B. SMITH · SAM HAWLEY · CHARLEY COINER

REX BEACH · EVELYN ZERN · LOUIS LIONNI · BEN SHAHN

WALLACE OSTRANDER · WILLIAM J. MILLER · PRESTON JENNINGS

BOB & BETTY GREIG · ERNIE ST.CLAIR · JED RIEHL

JACK HENRY · JUDGE PATRICK STONE · ROBERT LEE

JOSEPH CULLMAN · STUYVESANT WAINWRIGHT · WILLIAM LONG

ERNIE MALTZ · HOYT HOLLAND · ZENAS BLOCK

RALPH KUHN · JAMES O. JOHNSON · ANNA MAE KEENER

ROY CLEVELAND · CRAIG GREINER · DON RAY · WESLEY GILMAN

BROOK RUSSELL · AL ZWEIER · HENRY LANIER

HUGH MACNAIR KAHLER · SAMUEL N. PIERSON · RIPLEY ROPES

DICK BROWN · JACK RUSSELL · JOHN VOORHEES

ROBERT D. HALL · R. M. BRINKERHOFF · PHIL JONES

JIM LEISENRING · ED SENZ · DON HEROLD · ROBERT SEELEY

PAUL O'HAIRE · GEORGE SWAIN · LOU SCHAUER

OTTO LUTHER · FRED C. KELLY · IK SHUMAN

ALTHOUGH NOT NECESSARILY IN THE ORDER NAMED

—H.T.W. & E.Z.

NOTICE

THE views expressed in this book are those of the author, and do not necessarily reflect the policy of the publisher. As a matter of fact, the only policy of the publisher is to sell enough books to be able to retire from publishing and get into some business where he doesn't have to have dealings with every crackpot who happens to have access to a typewriter.

CONTENTS

THE WOMAN WHO THOUGHT
THIS YEAR THEY WOULD
SPEND THEIR VACATION TOGETHER
AT SOME NICE, BIG SEASIDE HOTEL

© 1941·N·Y·TRIBUNE INC.

How to Torture Your Wife

FOREWORD

by COREY FORD

I DON'T KNOW why anybody should write a foreword to a collection of H. T. Webster's fishing
cartoons. If there's one artist who needs no introduction, that would be Webbie. For years
people who fish have been clipping his drawings
out of newspapers and mailing them to other people who fish
(usually with some snide comment such as "What does this remind
you of, eh? Ha, ha!") and a foreword at this late date is about as
useful as a pair of waders with a hole in the seat.

But how about the people who don't fish? How about the people
who live with people who fish? What of the people who have to sit
on the bank and swat flies while the people who fish are fishing?
Isn't it about time somebody said a word or two about *them?*

So this is what this foreword is. This is a foreword for the people
the people who fish marry. Take a wife on a fishing trip. (And you
have only yourself to blame.) What does she get out of it? If she
strolls along the stream with her husband, she will spend her time
clambering over rocks to get his landing-net, or climbing balsam
trees to rescue the fly he has hung up on a back-cast. If she stays
and waits beside the car, she will get eaten by mosquitoes, or rained
on, or chased by a cow. If her husband doesn't catch anything, she
will have to listen all the way home to the reasons why. (The water
was too high, too low, too muddy, too cold, too unusual, etc.) If her
husband *does* catch anything, she'll have to cook it.

Nor is her ordeal limited to a few hours on a stream. The average
fishing trip ends on the afternoon of the last day of trout season,
and begins again the following morning. This gives the fisherman
almost twelve hours a year to shake hands with his wife, introduce
himself to any new members of his family who may have arrived
in the meantime, drop in at the office and look over his mail, and

get caught up on a little sleep before it is time to start getting his tackle in shape for next time.

Over the autumn and winter, to be sure, he might almost pass for a normal member of the community in good standing. His friends are encouraged. "Brown actually seems to be taking an interest in things again," they nod approvingly. "I'm glad you can talk something else besides fish, fish, fish," his wife sighs in relief. Occasionally his gaze will waver as he passes a goldfish store, or he will stand and turn a pencil sharpener for hours as he winds an imaginary reel. Perhaps you will notice a slight froth around the corners of his mouth when some unsuspecting guest, admiring the stuffed trout over the mantel, attempts to make table-conversation by remarking that he used to be a fisherman himself. "Yep," leaning back and joining his fingertips together reminiscently, "when I was a kid I used to get a kick out of digging clams. There's quite an art to digging clams...." But on the whole, he seems to have recovered from his mania entirely, chats quite normally with friends at the club, listens when they discuss automobiles or golf. "He even played a hand of bridge the other night," his wife confides proudly.

It is along about January, when the coal is getting low in the bin and the winds howl down the chimney, that the first fatal symptoms begin to appear. He will finger the pages of an old sporting-magazine uneasily, fidget in his chair, lay it aside with a sigh, pick up last year's fishing catalogue and pore over it with an increasing show of restlessness. His lips move silently, his fingers drum absently on the sides of the chair, his eyes shift from the pages, and he stares into space. His wife lays down her knitting and watches in silence as he rises from his chair with a mumbled excuse, shuffles upstairs to his bedroom with a faraway glassy expression in his eye, and takes down his fishing jacket from a peg in the attic. Reverently, he empties the pockets and pores alone over the holy relics: his last year's license, some tangled leaders, a handful of water-soaked matches, a button from his wading-suspenders, something unpleasant like old gravy in the bottom of his pocket (that's where that chocolate bar went to), and the key to his partner's car. Downstairs his wife shakes her head and returns resolutely to her knitting. She knows the telltale signs. It won't be long now.

The change shows more clearly in his face as February dawns. Now he makes no pretense of being civil to his family any longer. He excuses himself right after dinner and hurries upstairs to the attic, a fixed and purposeful gleam in his eye. Hour after hour, long after the rest of the household has retired, he sits alone in the dim light of a single candle, telling over his artificial flies like a rosary: big flies and little flies, dark flies and light flies, fluffy and sparse flies; flies tied on tens and twelves and fourteens, invisible flies, flies tied with quill-bodies, flies tied with fan-wings, flies tied with mole-fur, flies tied with helicopter wings, a cowbell, and a small electric light in the eye; Montreals and Quill Gordons and Pink Ladies and Royal Coachmen and Hackles and Hare's Ears and Sedges and Duns and Willows and Gnats. One by one he inspects each bright-colored lure, smooths its ruffled hackle gently, rewinds a loose strand of quill here or repairs a bit of floss-silk dressing there, brushes the wings soothingly, croons to it a little, and replaces it reluctantly at last in its compartment again, where it will remain during the rest of the year while he goes on taking all his fish on the same bedraggled Cahill he has been·using for three successive seasons.

March, and the honk of wild geese is in the air. Now there is a wild fanatic gleam in his eye. Night after night his wife sits downstairs alone and listens resignedly to the telltale snarl of a reel being unwound, the bump of furniture as he strings the freshly greased line from the bedpost to the bureau and across to the doorknob, the muffled oath as he forgets and trips over it on his way out. She knows it is only a question of time. Evidences mount daily: her sewing-basket is rifled for worsted and silk thread, a few more feathers are missing from her hat. The house reeks with the fumes of reel-oil, varnish for the rods, Muculin for the lines, cement for the ferrules, patching-glue for the waders. Conversation at the dinner table is limited to "I wonder whether a fan-wing Royal Coachman would do better in the Railroad Pool?" or "Dear, what did you do with my old fishing pants?"

A week before the start of the trip, the household is in a state bordering on frenzy. Nothing is anywhere. The fishing jacket is hidden from sight, the landing-net has been maliciously spirited away, someone has made off with his creel. Freshly-varnished rods dangle from the chandelier, wading-boots hang in the front hall, socks festoon the living-room fireplace, leaders are soaking in the bathtub. By the time the morning of the trip dawns, the head of the house is not on speaking terms with anyone else. Someone has deliberately, I said deliberately, opened his fly-box and taken out his favorite # 10 Quill Gordon. It does no good to locate the Quill Gordon stuck in the band of his hat. Who went and hid it in his hat?

All the way to the stream, the fisherman keeps the throttle pressed down to the floorboards, as though every other fisherman in the world were making for the same particular pool. The tires squawk to a halt, the fisherman dives out, and clambers into his waders, and starts walking away while assembling his rod. He pauses and glances vaguely at his wife as though he had never seen her before. "You wait here, dear," he calls over his shoulder. "I'm just going upstream a little ways. I'll be back in five or six hours, unless the fishing is good...."

Which is where this foreword comes in. This foreword is for the benefit of the Trout Widow, thus abandoned and left to shift for herself. It is sincerely hoped that she may find a crumb of comfort in these sympathetic pages. And meantime, while she is sitting on the bank and reading them, I'm just going a little ways upstream. I'll be back in five or six hours.

Unless the fishing is good....

TO HELL
WITH
FISHING

HOW TO DISPOSE OF DEAD FISH

A RECENT survey showed that roughly two-thirds of all fishermen never eat fish. This should surprise nobody. Fish is brain food. People who eat fish have large, well-developed brains. People with large, well-developed brains don't fish. It's that simple.

The question a fisherman faces, then, is how to get rid of the fish he has caught. There are several schools of thought on this problem.

The Pilgrim Fathers buried a dead fish in each hill of corn to make it grow. Unfortunately, few fishermen have access to cornfields. Most farmers would sooner have a cyclone.

Some fishermen try to palm off their catch on kindhearted friends and neighbors. Naturally, it doesn't take *those* folks long to learn that when a trout has been lugged around all day in a hot creel, it is poor competition for a pork chop.

Other methods of fish disposal are (1) stuffing them in a corner mailbox when nobody is looking, (2) hiding them under potted palms, (3) checking them at the Union Depot and throwing away the check, (4) hurling them from fast-moving cars on lonely roads late at night, (5) mailing them to the Curator of the Museum of Natural History, requesting an identification of the species and giving a phoney name and return address, and (6) baiting walrus-traps with them.

None of these methods is satisfactory. (1) is probably illegal, (2), (3), (4), and (5) are in lousy taste, and (6) brings up the problem of walrus-disposal. Walrus-disposal makes fish-disposal seem like child's play.

My friend Walt Dette throws back all the trout he catches in the Beaverkill, and keeps only chubs to feed to his seven Siamese cats. This is dandy for people who have (a) sense enough to put back trout for future sport and who also have (b) seven Siamese cats. Few fishermen have both.

Both, hell. *Either.*

[7]

Life's Darkest Moment

AIN'T IT THE TRUTH? NO

Fishermen are born honest, but they get over it.

When a fisherman is going to tell you about the big musky he caught, he knows you will subtract ten pounds to allow for his untruthfulness.

So he adds ten pounds to allow for your subtraction.

The other ten pounds he adds on account of being such a liar.

Then he adds five pounds for good measure because what is five pounds more or less on such a big fish?

As a matter of fact, he didn't even catch that musky. He found it floating belly-up.

It died laughing at a Hokum's DeLuxe Weedless Streamlined Hollow-ground Galvanized Non-skid Semi-automatic Husky-Musky Lure with Centerboard Optional, $1.50 at all sporting-goods stores.

Lizzie Greig, the Gal Fly-tier of the Angler's Roost, was born in Scotland on the River Tweed. It was too late at night to borrow the greengrocer's scales, so they used the one her father used for salmon.

She weighed 34 lbs., 5 ozs.

The Boy Who Made Good

HOW TO CATCH FISH WITH FLIES

SOME wiseguy once defined a fishing line as a piece of string with a worm on one end and a damn fool on the other.

This is a silly definition, of course—for many fishermen use flies instead of worms. They think it is more hoity-toity. If worms cost two bits apiece, and you could dig Royal Coachmen and Parmacheene Belles out of the manure pile, they would think differently. This is called human nature.

Fly fishermen spend hours tying little clumps of fur and feathers on hooks, trying to make a trout fly that looks like a real fly. But nobody has ever seen a natural insect trying to mate with a Fanwing Ginger Quill.

Of course, every once in a while a fly fisherman catches a trout on a trout fly, and he thinks this proves something. It doesn't. Trout eat mayflies, burnt matches, small pieces of inner tube, each other, caddis worms, Dewey buttons, crickets, lima beans, Colorado spinners, and almost anything else they can get in their fool mouths. It is probable they think the trout fly is some feathers tied to a hook. Hell, they're not blind. They just want to see how it tastes.

Trout flies are either wet flies or dry flies, depending on whether they are supposed to sink or float. If you ask a wet-fly fisherman why a natural insect would be swimming around like crazy under water, he gets huffy and walks away.

Many fishermen think trout are color-blind, but that is nothing to what trout think of fishermen.

AT THIS STAGE OF
THE PROCEEDINGS THE
REEL DROPS OFF THE
ROD ——————————

Life's Darkest Moment

HOW TO WADE A TROUT STREAM

NOTHING is so disturbing to the joys of trout-fishing as to step on a slippery rock while wading a stream and go hip boots over tincups. There are several ways of avoiding this. Some people wear nonskid chain devices attached to their boots. Some people wear stocking-foot waders and hobnailed or felt-soled shoes. Some people with more gray matter just stay the hell out of trout streams.

Statistics show that one-legged fishermen seldom fall down while wading. I only know one one-legged angler personally. He lost the other one while poking good-natured fun at a buzz saw, and had it replaced with an aluminum job, made by the Dodd Artificial Limb Company. He is very proud of it. When somebody suggested that he turn it in during an aluminum scrap drive, he indignantly refused.

"I don't give a good Dodd gam!" he said.

How to Torture Your Wife

WHY DUMB PEOPLE CATCH MORE TROUT
THAN SMART PEOPLE

Iғ ʏоu hang around Charley's Hotel Rapids on the Brodheads Creek, or Frank Keener's Antrim Lodge on the Beaverkill, and pay close attention to the inmates, you will notice that the lamer the brain, the heavier the creel.

The reason for this is very simple. When a fisherman gets to the stream he looks it over and decides where he would go if he were a fish. Then he takes out his worm can or his fly-box and decides which worm or which fly he would prefer if he were a fish.

Then he drifts his worm or casts his fly into the spot he has decided on. If he catches a fish, he is very proud, because he knows he thinks like a fish. And naturally, fishermen who think like fish catch more trout than fishermen who think like armadillos or duck-billed platypuses or mongooses.

Of course, the reason a fish thinks the way he does is that his brain is very tiny in relation to his body. So the tinier the fisherman's brain the easier it is for him to think like a fish, and catch trout right and left.

The same principle explains why fishermen with big mouths catch the most large-mouth bass, and fishermen with banjo eyes catch the most walleyed pike, and fishermen with jaundice catch the most yellow perch, and so forth.

The virgin sturgeon has never been caught on rod and reel.

The Thrill that Comes Once in a Lifetime

HOW TO TELL FISH FROM FISHERMEN

Hardly a day goes by at my office but that some damn fool wakes me out of a sound sleep to complain he has difficulty telling fish from fishermen. Actually, it is a simple matter, once you get the hang of it.

There are several methods of telling the difference. One way is to observe the subject while it is reading a newspaper. If its lips do not move, it is a fish.

The most dependable way is to carry a copy of *American Food and Game Fishes,* by Jordan and Everman. Anything not listed in the index is a fisherman.

A much tougher problem is how to tell small-mouth bass from large-mouth bass. Here are a few simple rules to remember:

Small-mouth bass like the cold, clear water of spring-fed ponds and swift streams. Large-mouth bass figure water is water.

Large-mouth bass think wobbling plugs look like crippled minnows. This just goes to show you.

Small-mouth bass adore spinner-and-fly combinations. Gollup Kuhn, the Champeen Liar of Lackawaxen, caught a small-mouth bass by trolling a privy-door hinge in the Delaware River. It is this sort of thing that makes the Anglers Club of New York blow its top.

Large-mouth bass hang around stumps and lily pads, passing the time of day. Small-mouth bass prefer rocky ledges. Ask them why and they hem and haw. Paradoxically, small-mouth bass fishermen tell bigger lies than large-mouth bass fishermen.

Incidentally, the flavor of a large-mouth bass is vastly improved by popping it into the garbage can and going out for dinner.

During severe droughts, the catfish buries itself in the mud. On him, it looks good.*

* Recently a man in East Liverpool, Ohio, hit his mother-in-law with a catfish. It got him nowhere.

Life's Darkest Moment

AIN'T NATURE NATURAL?

WHEN FISHERMEN come home from a day's fishing empty-creeled, and you say well, where are the fish, ha ha, they say look, bub, can't you get it through your thick skull there is more to fishing than catching fish.

But when you say what, for instance, they are stumped.

Sometimes they mumble around about getting next to nature. But the fact is, fishing has no more relation to nature than Spit-in-the-ocean with deuces, treys, and one-eyed face-cards wild.

Take trout fishing.

Trout are raised in hatcheries and fed on ground-up horses. They are not even allowed to have normal sex relations. When a boy trout starts sidling up to a girl trout, a couple of nature-lovers grab them and squeeze their milt and roe into a pan.

The little trout are kept in tanks until they're several inches long. Then they're loaded into nice natural tank-trucks and hauled out to a stream or pond and dumped in.

When they find there is no horse meat in the water, they go around gnawing at beer bottles, mattress springs, tin cans, old galoshes, worn-out girdles, Silver Doctors, and the other natural articles found in trout streams.

As a matter of fact, the most popular trout in America—the brown trout—isn't even natural to this continent. It was imported from Europe in 1884. If it knew how to get back there, it would probably go.

The only reason there is any trout fishing in most states is that Conservation Departments have learned to kick Mother Nature in the teeth every time she comes messing around.

When you hear a fisherman talking about the beauties of nature, you can rest assured he would not know the old lady if she knocked him down and sat on him.

And if you got a better idea, let's have it.

How to Torture Your Wife

ALL ABOUT GUIDES

No wonder normal people can't stand fishermen. Fishermen can't stand each other. They have to pay people to keep them company.

Guides are people who can stand anybody. For seven dollars a day and their keep, they will associate with fishermen. For eight dollars a day, who knows *what* they would do?

In the evening, guides sit around the campfire and spit in it. They like to hear the sizzle. After a day of fishing, it makes sense.

My friend Lyman Clark went moose-hunting. He asked his Indian guide what he should do. The guide took him to a clearing, and said,

"You sittum down on stump. Me blow in birchbark horn, makum noise like cow moose in heat. Bull moose, he hearum. Run like hell ketchum cow. Me keep on blowum horn. Bull moose runnum in clearing. You shootum. You shootum good. You no shootum, bull moose rapum guide."

Fishermen call guides "picturesque." Guides call fishermen "sports."

The other guides know what they mean.

Life's Darkest Moment

ALL ABOUT BIG-GAME FISHING

PEOPLE WHO are just taking up big-game fishing are called learners. People who know more about big-game fishing than anybody else put together are called Lerners.* This is so confusing that many people just throw up their hands and change the subject.

The only difference between big-game fishing and collecting old millstones is that millstones aren't slimy.**

In between fishing expeditions, big-game fishermen go around lifting Percheron horses off the ground and pulling loaded freight cars with their teeth. In the evening, they gather in small groups and feel each other's muscle.

Big-game anglers and fresh-water anglers sneer at each other. And why not?

* This is a pun, and refers to Mr. and Mrs. Michael Lerner, who invented horse-mackerel fishing.
** Contrary to popular misconception, whales are not fish. Otherwise, there is little to be said in their favor.

How to Torture Your Wife

THE LOW-DOWN ON WESTERN FISHING

THE PUBLISHER of this book, who has never been west of River-side Drive, insists there ought to be something in here about western fishing. He says there are plenty of fishermen in states like California and Omaha and Arizona who have two bucks and no sense of value.

My only experience in western fishing was a day spent on Puget Sound, sitting in Carl Cleveland's pappy's motorboat, drinking Yakima Valley applejack and trolling for king salmon. Due to some special quality of Yakima Valley apples, I am a bit hazy on the details.

As I recall, there was a lead sinker the size of a honeydew melon on the end of the line, just ahead of a metal wobbler and a large hook. The theory is, I believe, that the salmon swims over to have a look at the wobbler, and while doing so, collides with the sinker, is stunned, and floats belly-up to the surface.

I don't know what the hook is for, and I felt awful the next morning.

In general, I would say that western fishing is pretty much the same as eastern fishing, only sillier.

Life's Darkest Moment

THE TRUTH ABOUT IZAAK WALTON

I F YOU think *this* book is dull, go curl up with *The Compleat Angler, or The Contemplative Man's Recreation.* Then try to uncurl.

Of course, Izaak Walton wrote *The Compleat Angler* a long time ago. Even nonfishermen could not spell very good in those days.

The Compleat Angler is all about a character named Piscator. Later, in disgust, he became a stage director.

Izaak Walton pretended to be an expert on fishing. In his introduction, he refers to "the honest Angler." That's how much *he* knew.

The Compleat Angler is chock-full of useful information for fishermen. For example, in Part 1, Chapter IV, it says: "And next you are to notice, that the Trout is not like the Crocodile." Walton was observant.

In Chapter VIII, he tells of a man who caught a pike by using a mule as bait. Fortunately for Ike, it was several hundred years before anybody read beyond Chapter I.

In the same chapter, he also tells of a pike that bit a Polish girl's foot. Personally, I would prefer this type bait over mules.

I once knew a Polish girl in Hamtramck, Mich., who ▬▬▬▬▬

▬▬▬▬▬▬▬▬▬▬▬▬▬▬▬▬▬▬▬▬▬▬▬▬▬▬▬ *

not once but several times!

* Publisher's Note: This is Mr. Zern's first book. He has apparently never heard about postal regulations.

HOW TO TAKE PHOTOGRAPHS OF FISH

See diagram (drawn by author) below:

By the way, exactly who is this guy Webster?

THE COLLECTED ANGLING CARTOONS OF
H. T. WEBSTER

For a number of years now, and to the delight of several million readers of the New York *Herald Tribune* and other newspapers throughout America, H. T. Webster has been gently jabbing his pen at the foibles, follies, whims, eccentricities, and highly specialized insanity of fishermen.

Unfortunately, Mr. Webster is a well-rounded personality, so that he feels obliged to point out the peculiarities of bridge-players, bores, bankers, burglars, brokers, bartenders, bishops, and other subspecies of mankind as well—and the angling subjects pop up in his daily space at irregular and all-too-infrequent intervals. This makes it difficult to maintain a Webster scrapbook—and for a long time there has been a screaming need for a compilation of his best-loved fishing cartoons in one handy volume.

One of the beauties of a Webster cartoon is that it needs no interpretation or commentary—it's all right there, in black and white. Nevertheless, the publisher insisted that some text be included between the drawings, to keep them from sticking together. "The public be damned!" he said...and I am the type that knows which side his bread is buttered on. I hope that the remarks, most of which are thoroughly inappropriate and in questionable taste, won't interfere too much with your enjoyment of the drawings.

E. Z.

PLEASE NOTE that the obnoxiously successful angler in the upper left corner is not wearing waders—probably because she once wore a pair in front of a full-length mirror. If I ever got the job of eliminating sex as a factor in American life, my first step would be to compel all women under fifty to wear stocking-foot waders with felt-soled shoes. If this failed, I'd know I was licked, and hand in my resignation.

How to Torture Your Husband

Probably, deep in his heart, the kid feels a certain contempt for the fancy-pants fisherman with the elegant equipment.

Driving along beside a beautiful stretch of a closely posted stream one afternoon, Jack Rowles and I beheld a gentleman in a cashmere sport coat and neatly pressed doeskin slacks, seated languidly on a shooting stick on the bank and casting a fly, while his gentleman's gentleman stood by—presumably to disengage fish from the hook when necessary, change flies, announce callers, serve tea, etc.

This sight so unnerved us that we considered stopping the car and chucking some large, plebeian stones at the toff, but the evening rise was due to start shortly, and we had several miles to drive to public water.

The Thrill that Comes Once in a Lifetime

PERSONALLY, I can't understand the fanaticism of the dry-fly purist. Except under abnormal conditions, trout in eastern streams are easier to take with the artificial fly than with any natural bait I've ever tried—and, of course, a lot more fun. But if there were such a creature as an unbiased angler, I think he'd admit that in clear water flowing at normal levels during the season when natural flies are hatching, there's more skill and streamcraft involved in taking trout on a worm than in flimflamming them with a floater.

Fishing the lower Brodheads with Larry Madison one day, I saw a brown trout as long as your leg poke his head leisurely out of the water, take a large butterfly fluttering about ten inches above the surface, and slide back into the depths. When my hair had uncurled and I'd told Larry about this, we each caught a large butterfly, tied it with thread to a #14 hook on the end of a stout leader, and waded down opposite sides of the stream, letting the butterflies butterfly around at the ends of their tethers. For all the fish we caught by this ingenious trick, we might as well have been trolling Rangeley spinners from the back of a Fifth Avenue bus.

Life's Darkest Moment

A FLYTYING friend of mine recovered from a serious illness recently. Meeting him on the street, I said I was disappointed to see him up and around, as I had planned to see his wife the day after the funeral and buy some of the superb badger and blue dun rooster necks in his collection. He said it was just as well he'd pulled through, as his wife was opposed to his spending money to indulge as foolish a hobby as flytying, but on the other hand was one of those gals who simply can't resist a bargain. For years he had been coming home with a new neck and saying, "Look, dear! A $25 neck—and I got it for only $5!" He said I'd have got quite a shock at the prices his wife would have asked in all innocence.

It so happens that several of my other flytying acquaintances have been feeling rather poorly of late—and to protect myself, I'd like to inform their wives here and now that the best dry-fly neck in the world isn't worth a cent more than $10, even during wartime inflation.

THE REPAIR BILL
ON A TROUT ROD

How to Torture Your Husband

Every man has at least one chink in the armor of his honesty. I once knew an Episcopal bishop who stole bird dogs. And it's a rare stretch of water that doesn't look more inviting for a couple of "No trespassing" signs.

A well-known professional flytier once told me that her father, who lives beside a famous Scottish salmon river, had poached the preserved water all his life, and was the terror of every bailiff for miles around. On the old man's seventieth birthday, the owners sent word that henceforth he had their permission to fish their water, and would no longer be bothered by the wardens.

This action so demoralized the gaffer that he went into a profound funk and refused to go near the river for several months. When he appeared to be wasting away, his wife persuaded the owners to withdraw their devastating offer of immunity, and the old man took up his poaching where he had left off. The last I heard, he was well in his eighties, and still good for a brace of salmon every evening during the runs.

The Timid Soul

Fishing the Willowemoc last year, I rose a trout to my next-to-last-remaining Blue Spider, but left the fly in his jaw when I struck too hard.

I hated to lose that fly—good naturally-blue hackle is hard to come by—and so I rashly announced to my companions that I'd get it back the next morning. I also described the fish as at least a sixteen-incher. I could tell by the feel when he took the fly.

Jack Rowles, Founder and President of the Beaverkill Chub Club, denied hotly that (a) I could raise a trout that had a fresh hook in its jaw and (b) that I could judge the size of a trout by breaking off a fly in it, and we argued these points until the bartender started putting out the lights.

The next morning Jack went with me to the pool, and on the first cast of my only other Blue Spider a trout took the fly and was netted. The fish (a) had my original Blue Spider stuck in the corner of his jaw, and (b) was nine inches long.

We called it a draw.

Life's Darkest Moment

IF THIS kid has the wit of a Devon minnow, he will suggest that the kindly old codger go soak his head. In my opinion, Gramps is lying in his store teeth: if he'd ever risen that leviathan to a dry fly, and netted it, he'd have rushed for the clubhouse and started screaming for a taxidermist.

THE MONSTER TROUT

Life's Darkest Moment

I MET A man on the Bushkill one time who was carrying a portable radio. He said it was the only way he could catch the Sunday afternoon symphony concerts and still be out on a trout stream. He'd tune in a good concert, turn up the volume and set the radio on a rock beside a good pool. By intermission time he'd have worked that pool pretty thoroughly, and during the commercial he'd move on to the next one.

He said the music had a definite effect on the trout, despite theories that fish can't hear sounds in the air. He claimed that trout rose like crazy to Mozart, Haydn, and Vivaldi, but became nervous and irritable during a Brahms program, rising short if at all. Any Wagner composition would send them straight to the bottom, where they'd sulk—although a Beethoven quartet would bring them up again.

He said he personally admired the work of Shostakovich, but that brown trout were apparently conservative, and drew the line at Prokofieff. Also, that one of the best days he'd ever had was completely ruined in the midst of a terrific green drake hatch, when he accidentally tuned in a singing commercial and put down every trout for miles around.

The Unseen Audience

THERE are a number of preparations on the market which are sold on the pretext that they will repel insects. Possibly these are quite effective on praying mantises and boll weevils—but to mosquitoes, black flies, deer flies, sand flies, no-see-ums, and the other man-eating species, they are simply an *apéritif*. I once spent two unhappy days on the Esopus, sitting around a fisherman's hotel, with both eyes swollen tightly shut by black-fly bites, listening to less allergic anglers tell me how good the fishing was.

The sooner science stops fumdiddling around with atoms and molecules and starts concentrating on black flies, the sooner we will be getting somewhere.

Life's Darkest Moment

I THINK this is a very funny cartoon, because I suggested the idea to Mr. Webster. I expected it would be signed: "WEBSTER —IN COLLABORATION WITH ED ZERN, THAT DELIGHTFULLY CLEVER PRINCE OF GOOD FELLOWS." Instead, all I got out of it was a rather cavalier "plus Z," and in the wave of speculation as to the identity of "Z" that swept the United States and possessions, I came off a poor second to Joe Zilch.

How to Torture Your Wife

Sometimes this "thrill-of-a-lifetime" business can be overdone. My friend John M. once got both barrels at the same time, and it floored him. John's wife was due to have her first baby in a couple of days, but he figured he could get back from the Brodhead in a few hours, in case things started popping, so I met him at Analomink for the week end.

On Sunday, we fished the big flats above the island, and John landed a twenty-two-inch brown trout on a dry fly and light leader. It was the biggest trout by six or seven inches that John had ever caught, and when he'd stopped trembling, he hurried back to Charley's Hotel Rapids to display his prize. As he marched through the front door, holding the trout high for all to admire, Charley called from behind the bar, "Congratulations, John! Your wife had an eight-pound boy about an hour ago!"

John stopped dead in his tracks, and his jaw sagged. He looked at Charley and then he looked at the trout, and then he looked at Charley. Then he made a funny gurgling noise and flopped down hard on a handy chair. It was nearly an hour before he had recovered sufficiently to change his clothes and start driving home.

The Thrill that Comes Once in a Lifetime

THIS shows how well-meaning people go around messing up other people's lives. Up to the moment illustrated, the luckless laddie was perfectly content with his pole, string, and bent pin. From now on, he'll eat his heart out until he can own a $60 rod, a $20 reel, a $15 tapered line, and the expensive trimmings that go with them. But in order to get those items, he'll have to turn down his parents' pleas to stay on the farm, and go to make his fortune in the city. Since he has no special talents or abilities, and is not very bright, he'll spend forty years working his way up to be assistant manager of the shipping department. When his kids have grown up and married, he'll be able to afford a fairly good fishing outfit, but he'll be too decrepit to use it.

When I meet a country boy on the stream, and he starts eyeing my rod, I threaten to wallop his bottom with it. Some people don't know when they're well off.

The Thrill that Comes Once in a Lifetime

ACCORDING to my own statistical survey, there are exactly 749,-621 people in this country who work fifty weeks a year so that they can afford to go fishing for the other two weeks. And of this number, exactly 749,619 arrive at their favorite stream or lake to find that the water is too high, too low, too muddy, too clear, too cold, too warm, too something or too other for good fishing.

Of the other two people, one slips on a stone and breaks his leg in two places the first day, and the other is so flabbergasted that he upsets the canoe and loses his tackle.

Life's Darkest Moment

PROBABLY the well-intentioned host is in the advertising business. There is an unwritten but quite rigid rule around advertising agencies that, wherever a fishing scene is illustrated, the tackle should be as ill-assorted as possible.

If you will find me an advertising illustration of a fishing scene in which the artist has not put a bait-casting reel on a flyrod, or vice versa, or in which a character is not flyfishing with a plug rod, or some similar incongruity, I will send you a brand-new, soft-iron hobnail free of charge.

Life's Darkest Moment

IN CASE you've ever wondered why so many trout fishermen beat their wives, here's one good reason.

AN AUDIENCE OF THREE
VETERAN DRY FLY FISHERMEN

How to Torture Your Husband

AND IF you're still wondering, here's another.

How to Torture Your Husband

AND another!

How to Torture Your Husband

Aɴᴅ ᴀɴᴏᴛʜ—what's that? It's all perfectly clear to you? You're quite sure? Very well then, let's get along to another topic.

How to Torture Your Husband

PERSONALLY, I don't get the point of this cartoon. As far as I can see, it's an ideal honeymoon, and I don't know what Mr. Webster could be driving at. I spent my honeymoon fishing for small-mouth bass. I had to. The trout season had ended.

THE HONEYMOON

Life's Darkest Moment

HERE Mr. Webster shows how a seemingly kind act can wreck several lives:

The kid retrieves the leader and fly, only to discover that in order to handle nine feet of leader and a dry fly, he needs at least a $20 rod. In order to get the twenty, he holds up a filling station and inadvertently assassinates the proprietor, who leaves a wife and eleven children in utter, abject poverty. The kid is sent to a reformatory, where he contracts whooping cough and dies. His parents commit suicide from grief and shame. Meanwhile, the guy who was too lazy to hunt for his leader and fly in the brush pile is going around telling all and sundry what a helluva generous fellow he is.

The Thrill that Comes Once in a Lifetime

THE MOST successful wet fly I ever used was an ancient Royal Coachman. I cut the wings off, leaving just the stump, and all but a few wisps of hackle, and fished it as a nymph. When several dozen Beaverkill trout had chewed it to a frazzle, I stuck it together again with collodion. It looked absolutely ghastly, and worked better than ever.

If I can find a dog and an owl, I'll give the guide's pattern a try. It *sounds* good. (Incidentally, H. T. Webster has a genuine blue dun dog. I tried to persuade him that there was a market, among flytiers, for the combings, but he said he'd rather keep his dealings with the pup on a noncommercial basis.)

Life's Darkest Moment

PERSONALLY, I am opposed to having fish mounted. This may be because I've never caught one large enough to justify such exhibitionism, or it may be because a moose head on the wall of the Yale Club once winked at me, and I've never fully recovered. (Yale men are bad enough, but Yale moose are intolerable.)

Ernie Maltz, the Mad Angler of Riverside Drive, once broke up a beautiful friendship when a fishing companion said his wife had just had a twelve-pound baby, and Ernie suggested having it mounted. But shucks, he may have been only kidding.

How to Torture Your Wife

Possibly the shortage of pipe-cleaners will be ended by the time this book appears, and the fine Websterian flavor of the cartoon will be lost.

But it will still be a reminder of the marvelous variety of things that accumulate in a well-used fishing jacket. Ordinarily, I carry the following items in mine—most of them to no purpose whatsoever:

2 boxes of dry flies
2 boxes of wet flies
1 box of nymphs
1 box of streamers
1 spare reel with line
1 bottle of reel-oil
1 fishing knife with disgorger
1 fishing scales
1 stream thermometer
1 tin of fly dope
1 head net
1 bottle of dry-fly oil
1 specimen bottle for collecting nymphs and flies
1 wader-repair kit
1 gut-cutter
1 pad of line dressing
1 packet of strip-lead
1 tube of wetting-agent for leaders
1 pair of sun glasses
1 pack of cigarettes
1 tobacco pouch
2 pipes
1 package pipe-cleaners
1 lighter
1 bottle of collodion
1 leader-case
1 magnifying glass for examining stomach contents of fish

There are probably other items I can't recall at the moment, and until some manufacturer devises a jacket with more than the customary six or eight pockets, I shall continue to spend the better part of each fishing day digging around in my jacket looking for some gadget which my grampaw, who thought nothing of catching a hundred-odd brook trout in a day, never heard of. The lucky stiff.

The Thrill that Comes Once in a Lifetime

Judging from my own experience, I should guess that this cartoon was the first panel of a "strip," and that Mr. Webster was somehow sidetracked before he could finish it. In Panel #2, the kid makes a final lunge for the grasshopper, which grasshops away, causing the kid to fall on his face and scare the daylights out of every trout in the pool. I don't know what happens in subsequent panels of the strip, but I do know that catching 'hoppers is a lot more difficult and strenuous than catching trout.

(I've heard that if you get out early in the chill of the morning, before sunup, grasshoppers are numb with cold, and it's a simple matter to pick them off the bushes. Personally, I'd rather use artificial flies, and stay in bed 'til a decent hour.)

Life's Darkest Moment

THERE's alleged to be an extra satisfaction involved in catching trout on flies of one's own manufacture, but I've never noticed it. I tie my own flies because it keeps me out of mischief on long winter evenings and results in better flies than I can get from commercial sources. Also it enables me to invent all sorts of new patterns with which to confound the traditionalists and standpatters. (I doubt if the fly has ever been tied that was too freakish or fraudulent to take fish under certain conditions—and there are times when only the freak is effective. At least, I can't recall ever seeing a hatch of natural Fanwing Royal Coachmans.)

And since the kid brought a dog into the discussion, I might mention the guy who takes his Chespeake Bay Retriever on all his salmon-fishing trips. He takes the dog out in the canoe with him, and when he ties into a big bruiser that goes to the bottom and sulks, he boots the dog overboard and lets it swim around in the vicinity of the sulking salmon. This invariably starts the fish moving, and fast. (Apparently the salmon takes the dog for a fish-fancying seal on the prowl.)

This same character scorns trout as trout fishermen scorn suckers and carp. He claims that when he's fishing a salmon river, and wants a nice trout or two for the pan, he ties a six-foot leader, with a couple of wet flies attached, to his dog's tail. Then he throws a stick into the stream and tells the dog to fetch it. When the dog comes back to shore with the stick, he says, it is invariably towing a brace of trout.

And mind you, this guy is a pillar of the Methodist Church.

The Thrill that Comes Once in a Lifetime

I CAUGHT my first trout at the age of six, while poaching a private mountain stream in West Virginia. It was a good five inches long, and weighed upward of an ounce. I might have caught a larger one, but the owner came by and suggested I scram. He let me keep the trout to prove my prowess to my parents, but on the way back to the hotel I lost it.

Life's Darkest Moment

Speaking of fishermen's camps. I'm one of that decadent breed that likes them to have a modicum of modern conveniences. This is simply a matter of habit and upbringing. With a different background, I might feel like Gollup Kuhn, the Champeen Rassler, Raconteur, and Bee-liner of Pike County, Pa.

Gollup once forsook his homestead on the banks of the Delaware and went to visit a distant relative in the city. I asked him what he thought of city ways. "Durn little!" Gollup allowed, with fastidious indignation. "I never seen such unsanitary people. Why, they even got the privy right inside the house!"

Life's Darkest Moment

OF COURSE, Mr. Webster's only kidding about the old-timers being put to shame, as a rule, by the youngsters. The more years of experience, the smellier the creel.

I recall one day on the Brodheads, when I worked for an hour trying to put my dry fly over a rising fish. It was a long cast, and a tricky current kept dragging the fly out of the tiny eddy where the trout was feeding. Also, there was no room for a back cast, and I lost several precious fanwings in the trees that crowded the bank. When an elderly angler came by, I suggested he have a try at the inaccessible brownie. The stranger stepped into the stream, made a few false casts, and dropped a Pink Lady on the trout's nose. When he had netted the fish and released it, I asked him if there wasn't some secret to his success.

"There is indeed," he said.

"Would you mind telling *me* that secret?" I said.

"Of course not," he said. "It's really too simple for words."

"What is it?" I said.

"Just fish for fifty years," he said.

The Thrill that Comes Once in a Lifetime

THE PRESEASON fever that assails fishermen is too familiar to require any comment whatsoever.

Unfortunately, in the eyes of a publisher there is something unseemly—or at least unprofitable—in the sight of a blank page. A publisher figures that if a page has writing on it, somebody will pay him good money for the privilege of reading it.

And unless you borrowed this book, you're a case in point.

However, just to humor the Appleton-Century Company, here is a completely irrelevant story about Jim Deren, genial prop. of the Angler's Roost, who used to tote a Colt Woodsman while fishing, in order to shoot water snakes. Jim has taken a dim view of water snakes ever since he learned that they eat trout which might otherwise help to stink up his creel.

Several years ago, while wading the Willowemoc, Jim failed to notice that he had worked his way into a posted stretch of the stream. Suddenly the irate landowner rushed out onto a cable footbridge that spanned the stream a hundred feet above Deren. He had a shotgun, probably loaded with rock salt, and to express his irk, he fired both barrels high over Jim's head.

Naturally, Deren was startled, but retained sufficient composure to whip out his elegant gat and send a couple of slugs whistling past his annoyer's ear. The gentleman dropped his shotgun into the stream and withdrew, compensating for a lack of aplomb by sheer velocity.

Later, Deren was torn between thankfulness that he didn't have to account to a jury for a corpse, and chagrin at his faulty marksmanship. "There must have been a lot of cross wind," he alibied.

DAYLIGHT
AHEAD
———

© 1942 · N.Y. TRIBUNE INC.

The Thrill that Comes Once in a Lifetime